EASE

— AND —

FLOW

LAURA B. CALBERT

Balboa Press books may be ordered through booksellers or by contacting:

Balboa Press
A Division of Hay House
1663 Liberty Drive
Bloomington, IN 47403
www.balboapress.com
844-682-1282

Because of the dynamic nature of the Internet, any web addresses or links contained in this book may have changed since publication and may no longer be valid. The views expressed in this work are solely those of the author and do not necessarily reflect the views of the publisher, and the publisher hereby disclaims any responsibility for them.

ISBN: 978-1-9822-7011-7 (sc)
ISBN: 978-1-9822-7012-4 (e)

Library of Congress Control Number: 2021911956

Print information available on the last page.

Balboa Press rev. date: 08/04/2021

BALBOA.PRESS
A DIVISION OF HAY HOUSE

INTRODUCTION

Ease and Flow is incredibly unique! Its recipes are flavorful, fun, and easy to prepare. It will ignite a passion for food and is bound to create an atmosphere where your imagination will flourish. With the use of this cookbook comes the ability to comprehend what it means to cook intuitively and an opportunity to experience intuitive cooking firsthand.

Ease and Flow will remind you of the many benefits of having fun as you develop your intuition by trusting your inner guidance. This occurs naturally the more you practice the art of choosing what works best for you. Every delicious recipe in this cookbook is your personal invitation to perfect your art with ease and flow.

Ease and Flow allows you to choose how much of each ingredient is just enough. Instead of providing you with specific measurements and telling you which pots or pans to use, this book will let you decide based on how many servings you want to prepare. Are veggies chopped with a food processor or a knife? If you find chopping veggies with a knife to be therapeutic and think it makes cooking a much more pleasurable experience, even fun, then that answers your question! Think about it: shouldn't cooking be just that easy?

Ease and Flow was created to teach readers to trust their abilities to cook intuitively while having fun in the kitchen. Using this cookbook will add a pinch of that creative spark back into your meals and even your relationships, as you explore endless opportunities with every recipe. This book is great for both beginners and pros who are in search of innovative recipes. It is ideal for family dinners, date nights, cooking with children or friends, and so much more!

Ease and Flow is an interactive cookbook. After each recipe, you'll find a space where you, your family, and your friends can write down your own creations. A few delectable nuggets have been left along the way; when these are incorporated, suddenly, like magic, you level up the energy on each recipe. You will taste and see that your creations are oh so good when you're getting down in the kitchen. So join me on this adventure of *Ease and Flow*.

Energy Work

Choose a recipe that excites and inspires you! Then, you and your sous-chef will want to review the "Energy Work" section for the delectable nuggets I mentioned above. Energy work is a form of prayer that spiritually aligns your energy with everything you prepare. It is speaking life over the experience you are about to have and into the meal you are going to prepare. This practice will not only ensure that you'll have fun but also guarantee that each dish comes out just as good as you imagined it would.

Your Creation

Ease and Flow encourages you to make each and every recipe your very own and provides you the space to do so. The "Your Creation" note area is there for you to write the ingredients you chose, how much you used, and the cooking time. As you see, there are no strict rules or must-follows, just helpful hints and suggestions.

One significant suggestion you will find in just about every recipe is *enjoy*, which is defined as "to have for one's use or benefit: experience; to take delight, pleasure, or satisfaction in an activity of occasion." I believe that this describes with sheer perfection all of the desirable traits you should embrace whenever you step into your kitchen. Have fun creating and trusting your inner guidance, and before you know it, you will find that you to have the innate ability to be a creator too.

Mindful Suggestions

When prepping, always wash your veggies well. I like to allow them to soak in cool water with a little apple cider vinegar for a bit, then I give them a good rinse and pat dry. When using salt, less is more, and salts from the ocean are much healthier than those containing iodine. In these recipes, I used pink Himalayan sea salt.

I was a vegetarian at the time, so all of my meals calling for protein or meat are prepared with veggie protein. Veggie proteins require less cooking time; if you prefer to use chicken, beef, poultry, or fish, please always make sure to cook until done.

If you're new to the game, deciding which pot or pan to use may be challenging. Just practice your innate visualization abilities to determine if what you are about to prepare will fit while allowing you to stir without food spilling all over your stove. In other words, the more you intend to prepare, the larger the pot or pan you'll need.

Timing is everything, they say, so when you want to know exactly how long something needs to cook, set a timer. When I bake, I place my dish in the middle of the oven, and 350 degrees is my sweet spot. I usually cook my stovetop-prepared meals over medium-high heat or a low simmer. There's no pressure, though: simply allow your eyes and ears to be your guide!

SOUL FOOD TACOS

These are not your momma's tacos! They are the result of the mother of invention, as these delicious tacos are imaginatively prepared from the previous night's leftovers. They are pressed down and shaken together and running over with flavors from the motherland. One taste and, well, you know what it will make you want to do!

Energy Work

Your energy is everything, and the mindset you're in while cooking will reflect in every meal. So, prior to preparing this meal, I want you to recite these words: "I will enjoy this process of creating, and the food that I prepare will be nourishment for my body. Each step I take will be full of ease and flow and divinely guided. I will have fun, and this time will be used strictly for my enjoyment! As I prepare this meal, I will allow my energy to flow, and I will cook with pure love and appreciation." Now that that is done, put on some music for your enjoyment and try something new. Make it fun—let's get to it!

Fried Cabbage

red and green cabbage
sweet onion
fresh minced garlic
bouillon (I used Veggie)
Creole seasoning
crushed red pepper
Butter (I used Country Crock Plant Butter)

1. Wash, then thinly slice the cabbage and onion. Place a portion of the cabbage in a bowl for your coleslaw.
2. Heat your oil in your favorite pan. When it gets hot, add your onion. Stir it a bit, then add your garlic and bouillon.
3. When the onion becomes translucent, add remaining cabbage along with the Creole seasoning and crushed red pepper.
4. Allow the mixture to simmer on low until the cabbage becomes tender, stirring it every now and then to make sure you don't cook the crunch out!

Caribbean Candied Yams

yams
Country Crocks Plant Butter
dark brown sugar
Caribbean jerk seasoning
cumin powder
turmeric powder
crushed red pepper
salt

1. Wash and peel your yams. Pat them dry with a clean dry cloth or paper towel, then slice or dice them evenly and set aside.

2. Now, add your butter to your other favorite pan, and as soon as it has melted, add your brown sugar, allowing it to become creamy. This process only takes a minute or two.

3. Now, add all your spices and seasonings to your mixture; remember, salt is a flavor enhancer, so a little bit goes a long way.

4. Add the yams to your pan. Cover and allow them to cook until just tender; if you leave them too long, they will become mashed potatoes. If you can easily pierce them with a fork, they are good to go. Add some salt if necessary, give them another stir, leave them uncovered, and set them aside.

Coleslaw

fresh pineapple
shredded cabbage reserved from fried cabbage
cilantro
mayonnaise (I used Vegenaise)
salt
avocado

1. Dice your pineapple into tidbits or small chunks, then add it to the bowl with the cabbage.

2. Roughly chop the cilantro, then add it to the bowl. Give the slaw a bit of a mix, then stir in some mayonnaise and a little salt for flavor.

3. Slice the avocado for garnish—its creaminess tends to complement the flavor. Smells delicious. We're almost there!

Corn Taco Shells

Country Crocks Plant Butter
yellow or white corn taco shells
avocado slices

1. To a pan you don't mind frying in, add some butter. Either warm lightly or pan-fry the taco shells hard as you like. Remember, it's all about you!

2. Fill the shells first with your fried cabbage and candied yams. Top them off with a bit of your slaw, then crown them with a slice of avocado. You know what to do next … enjoy!

Your Creation

ELEVATION PIZZA BOWL

This one-pan meal is loaded with flavor and is definitely easy to prepare. This dish is a lighter version of regular delivery-style pizza, and you will enjoy it even without the crust. Each bite is packed with the creaminess of melted cheese and the sweet crunch of fresh veggies. It will elevate your taste buds to new heights!

Energy Work

The energy you put in is the energy you will receive! What you believe to be true will be, so use these words to ensure you are in alignment. I make choices that are healthy and that my body deserves. Cooking healthier options is fun and easy to do. I choose to enjoy the process and create new healthy habits that align with me and my needs. Mindful cooking is not about completely eliminating the urge to eat the foods that you enjoy; it is about making healthier choices and creating new ways to enjoy them. As old habits flow out, new ones flow in! Make sure you feel these words you have just recited.

Veggies

green cabbage
green bell pepper
onion
mushrooms

1. OK, let's get to it! Wash your veggies well and pat dry.
2. Next, slice each veggie the thickness you prefer.
3. After slicing veggies, place everything in a bowl and set aside.

Meat

protein (I used veggie pepperoni and veggie chicken tenders)
Italian seasoning
salt
nonstick cooking spray

1. Now let's prep the meat! If your meat option is already precooked (such as veggie meats and/or pepperonis), you can skip down to assembling your pizza bowl; but if the meat is raw, please continue.
2. If the portions of the meat are not already cut into small sections, feel free to cut them into bite-sized chunks. Place them in a bowl, then add your Italian seasoning and salt.
3. After you do this, spray your pan with oil, place on your stovetop, and preheat over medium heat. Toss raw meat into pan and cook until golden brown in color and completely cooked inside. Remove meat from pan and let it rest; this will allow it to retain its juices.

Pizza Bowl

reduced-sugar pizza sauce
mozzarella (I used violife)

1. Let's build your pizza bowl! Select a large pan or skillet with a lid, coat with cooking spray, and place on medium heat. Toss the veggies in all at once and allow them sauté. Watch your veggies while mixing them around in the pan a bit to ensure they cook evenly. Keep in mind there are more ingredients to be added to this cook time, and the longer you cook these veggies, the softer they will get. In other words, limit your sauté time if you like your veggies crunchy!

2. Now toss in your prepped meat, along with the precooked meat options and the pizza sauce. The more sauce you add, the saucier it will be, so if you're a saucy person, go for it!

3. OK, now let's stir this deliciousness well, cover, and allow to simmer on low heat. After a minute or two, sprinkle your cheese on top, cover until melted, and serve. Bon appetit!

Your Creation

ABUNDANCE BURRITO BOWL

This bowl is bold, fun, and vibrant. It will take your taste buds on an amazing adventure! It's satisfying from the very first bite to the very last, and great for meal prep or just a light dinner. The choice is yours.

Energy Work

Have you ever wondered why, throughout time and from culture to culture, before and/or after the cooking of a meal, there is some form of energy work done, whether it be in the form of prayer, affirmation, song, or chant? This alone should let you know the importance of ensuring that your energy is in alignment with what you are preparing to eat and that you are in the spirit of gratitude, radiant health, love, and abundance. Before we cook this meal, I want you and the person you are cooking with, or you by yourself should this be the case, to create your own form of energy balancing. Make it fun and make it your own. It can be as simple or as detailed as you would like. Create an energy of balance, ease, flow, love, gratitude, and creativity. Then watch as it transmutes the preparation process of your meal. When dinner is served, your senses become enhanced, and you find yourself enjoying it on levels you never have experienced before!

Rice

brown rice
veggie bouillon

1. Add water and rice to your pot. The size of the pot depends on the amount of rice you will be preparing. Feel free to follow the directions on the package of rice you've decided to use.
2. Once the water and rice have come to a boil, add the veggie bouillon. Bouillon tends to be a little salty, so again, depending on the amount you are preparing, use sparingly. My trick is to taste the rice during the cooking process. Brown rice will take considerably more time to cook than white rice, and the texture will be firmer. If the rice is done before all the water has boiled out, you can rinse, drain, and place it back on the unheated stove to sit.

Protein

onion
nonstick cooking spray
minced garlic
protein (I used Morning Star Fiesta Crumbles)
cumin powder
chili powder
salt
paprika powder
cilantro

1. Chop onion into small chunks.

2. Preheat pan and coat with your oil of choice, then toss in the onion, garlic, and veggie crumbles or ground meat. Remember, it's your choice!

3. Then go ahead and add the seasonings. However, if you are not familiar with those suggested, give them a little taste, and allow their flavors to be your guide as to how much of each you desire to add.

4. Using a spatula, mix the ingredients and let them simmer, occasionally mixing them so that everything is evenly cooked. I like mine a little crispy, so I only allow them to simmer a few minutes. (Side note: If you choose the veggie crumbles, their texture becomes more like meat the longer they cook!)

Corn Salsa

red onion
corn
black beans
lime
salt

1. Chop red onion and toss into a bowl.

2. Fresh corn is my favorite, but frozen or canned works as well. Drain the corn well to ensure there is no water left, then toss it into your bowl with the onion.

3. Black beans may also be canned; just make sure you rinse and drain them well before adding to the bowl with your other ingredients.

4. Squeeze in the lime, add your salt, and stir. Now, place the bowl in the fridge to chill.

Veggies

lettuce
tomato
red, yellow, and orange peppers
purple cabbage
Thoroughly wash your veggies, then chop them all into the size you desire … as you like!

Burrito Bowl

1. After all steps have been completed and the crumbles and your rice are done, you may begin plating your delicious meal! First, place the lettuce in the bottom of your serving dish.

2. Top the lettuce with rice. Next comes the crumbles, then the salsa, then sprinkle it with your rainbow of chopped veggies.

3. Feel free to top the bowl with your other favorite condiments, such as guacamole, sour cream, or even fiesta dressing—and enjoy!

Your Creation

POWER POTATOES AND VITALITY FRITTATA

Bold, full of flavor, and healthy, this dish is great for brunch, lunch, or even dinner, if you're anything like me. Have fun and feel free to express your creativity with this meal. The frittata is loaded with flavor and can literally be filled with any ingredients that makes your heart happy and your mouth water! It's sure to have everyone coming back for more. You will be pleasantly surprised to find that children enjoy this way of eating their veggies. So, let's dive in!

Energy Work

Free yourself from worry and enter a space of fulfillment. Cooking is a fun way to express your creativity and a cool way to explore endless opportunities. There are no rules, only choices. Release any anxiety or tension by taking the time to make the choices that you desire. Repeat these words out loud or mentally: *This is fun! I have the freedom to choose foods that are healthy for me. Everything I create is unique. I cook the foods I enjoy and enjoy the foods that I cook. I make great choices, and I trust the decisions I make!*

Power Potatoes

potatoes (I used russet)
red and yellow peppers
garlic
onion
Butter (I used Country Crocks Plant Butter)
salt
curry powder
paprika
black pepper

1. First, wash all your veggies well and pat dry. Dice potatoes into small cubes, then chop peppers, garlic, and onion into desired size.

2. Coat skillet with butter. Allow it to preheat on medium high, then toss in all your veggies and seasonings.

3. With a spatula, mix ingredients well to ensure that everything is coated with seasonings and oil, allowing them to sizzle a bit so the potatoes become a little crispy. Flip ingredients over by sections as you would a pancake, allowing them to sit uncovered and flipping occasionally.

4. Your potatoes should be lightly browned and the veggies translucent in color. Reduce heat to low and cover until tender.

Vitality Frittata

ground protein (I used Soyrizo)
spinach or kale
green onion
egg (I used Just Egg)
salt
black pepper
paprika
garlic powder
cheese (I used Chao)
Nonstick cooking spra

1. Preheat oven to 350 degrees.

2. Bring a pan to medium heat. Add the ground protein and cook to desired texture. (If using ground meat, add a little oil to pan; cook well until done).

3. Wash veggies and pat dry. Chop as desired and place in a medium bowl.

4. To the bowl, add Just egg, salt, and seasonings. (Keep in mind that the more veggies you use, the less egg you will taste).

5. Next, add the cheese and cooked meat; stir well.

6. Spray a square nonstick baking pan with oil, to ensure it does not stick. (the size of your bake pan will be determined by how many servings you're preparing) and pour mixture in. Bake until eggs are fluffy and fully cooked. I love the toothpick test! This is when you insert a toothpick into the middle of the dish; if it comes out dry, you're good to go.

7. Remove from oven and let cool before you cut and serve with your potatoes. Feel free to top with salsa or your favorite sour cream and enjoy!

Your Creation

MINDFULLY BALANCED BREAKFAST SKILLET

Fuel your body mindfully with this breakfast skillet. It's simple, quick, easy, and definitely delicious! This meal can be easily prepped in one pan and is full of nutrients. It will show you how simple breakfast can be and still be packed with beautiful and bold flavors. Yep, we are keeping it simple and taking this to a whole 'nother level!

Energy Work

Be mindfully engaged, take your time, and enjoy the cooking process. Everything in life is flying by at the speed of light; it seems we're always in a rush, and that energy is transferred into everything that we do. While preparing your meal, I want you to take some time to focus on the desired outcome of not just the food but the whole experience, whether you're alone or sharing it with someone else. Bring *love* back into the experience of cooking. Mindfully tune into the creativity of it all. Release the energy of it being a task or a chore and replace that with joy!

Pan-Fried Potatoes and Sautéed Kale

potatoes (I used russet)
ground protein (I used Morning Star Breakfast Sausage)
Nonstick cooking spray
paprika
butter (I used Country Crock Plant Butter)
kale
salt
cheese (I used Violife Cheddar)

1. Chop potatoes and desired protein into cubes; set aside.

2. Preheat skillet; coat bottom with desired oil and then add your potatoes, protein, and paprika. Toss them around in pan on medium/high heat until golden in color, then reduce heat to low and cover.

3. Wash kale; pat dry, then chop into smaller portions.

4. Move potatoes to one side of the skillet and add kale on the opposite side. Sprinkle kale with salt and add a little water on top to help with steam. Toss the kale around a bit and cover until both potatoes and kale are tender. Go ahead and taste it; that's the only way to know if it's to your liking.

5. Sprinkle potatoes with cheese. Cover to allow the cheese to melt.

Scrambled Eggs

butter (I used Country Crock Plant Butter)
eggs (I used Just Egg)

1. Preheat pan on medium heat.
2. Coat bottom of pan with butter. Allow butter to melt, then toss in the eggs and scramble.

Breakfast Skillet

1. Once eggs are done, toss in the middle of skillet with the potatoes and kale.
2. Place the whole skillet in the middle of table with a side of tortillas, toast, pancakes, or fruit. If you're on the go, wrap it in a tortilla or a warm piece of naan, or put it in your favorite to-go container. Whatever you decide, make sure you enjoy!

Your Creation

FOLLOW YOUR HEART
BEAN BURGER

Take your taste buds to new heights with this mile-high Mexican-inspired veggie bean burger—a great source of protein and full of nutrients! Follow your heart and let your creativity inspire each step.

Energy Work

Feel free to read this affirmation out loud or to yourself. I have the innate ability to create delicious food and the freedom to be as creative as I desire. The food that I cook comes from the heart, and I genuinely enjoy the process. Each ingredient I add is just enough and is perfect in its own way. Food is unique, and cooking allows me to express myself in a loving and compassionate manner. I enjoy the creation process and how it allows me to be me!

Bean Burger

mixed dry beans
canned chickpeas, drained
onion
cilantro
spicy ground protein (I used Soyrizo)
salt
tapioca flour
Non stick cooking spray

1. Soak beans overnight. After soaking, remove any small foreign particles. Rinse beans in a strainer, pour them into your pot, and cover with cool water. Remember, the size pot will depend on how much you decide to cook. Overcooking your beans will cause your burger to be mushy, so to acquire the perfect texture, you will need to keep a close eye on them during the cooking process.

2. Set your stovetop to medium high and allow your beans to cook while covered, stirring occasionally. When they come to a roaring boil, give them another good stir before lowering your temp to medium low. Allow them to continue simmering until slightly tender.

3. After beans are cooled, pour them into your food processer along with the drained chickpeas, onion, cilantro, Soyrizo (or the well-cooked protein of your choice), salt, and some tapioca flour. The flour acts as a binding agent; add a tablespoon at a time until your bean burger patties reach your desired consistency. Pulse the mixture to ensure that you don't create a paste; it should resemble the consistency of meat loaf.

4. After this process is complete, coat hands with flour and begin to form patties and place them on parchment paper.

5. Preheat pan with cooking oil on medium high and place patties into pan to cook. Make sure to leave enough space between each burger so they cook evenly and you have room to flip them.

Cashew Nacho Cheese

The more nutritional yeast you add, the cheesier the flavor will be. The more tapioca flour, the thicker it will be. Turmeric, while adding flavor, will also give your cheese sauce its cheddar-like color. Onion powder and salt will add another layer of flavor, and the nut milk will lend a creamy consistency.

raw cashews
nutritional yeast
tapioca flour
turmeric powder
salt
onion powder
unsweetened nut milk (I used cashew)

1. Soak cashews overnight. Rinse, drain, and place into a blender along with the other ingredients. Blend until the mixture is smooth.

Assembly

avocado
tomato
onion
purple cabbage
lime
fresh cilantro
cumin
hamburger buns

1. Clean and chop veggies to desired size. Halve lime.
2. Mix half the chopped tomato with chopped avocado and juice from the lime to create an easy, chunky guacamole. Add chopped fresh cilantro, cumin, or any seasonings that you desire.
3. Halve buns and toast in the oven. Once done, build your burger and enjoy!

Your Creation

_____

_____

_____

_____

_____

_____

_____

_____

_____

_____

_____

_____

_____

_____

_____

_____

_____

_____

_____

UNIVERSAL PASTA

Let your creativity explode! This dish was created with leftover sauces created the week before, and you can do the same! It's a blend of two sauces, veggies, pasta, and vegan Italian sausage—a fun twist on the well-known prepackaged hamburger meal. This one has elements of flavor that the old-time favorite will never be able to compete with!

Energy Work

Don't overthink the process, and don't worry about *what if it turns out all wrong*. Remember, there is no wrong; there are only choices! Take a few minutes to think about how you desire your meal to turn out. Visualize the outcome of your meal. See and taste it turning out just like you imagined. Feel good about the decisions you made that contributed to the creation of the meal that you desired. Have fun and enjoy the process. Visualization is key!

Sauce 1

cumin powder
crushed red pepper
black pepper
allspice
coriander
salt
bay leaves
cinnamon stick
onion
fresh minced garlic
tomatoes
vinegar
water

1. In a bowl, mix all dry ingredients except the bay leaves and cinnamon stick.

2. Chop onion and toss in a pan on medium heat with the minced garlic and sauté until translucent in color.

3. Puree tomatoes in a blender or food processor and pour into the pan. Add the dry seasonings along with the vinegar, bay leaves, and cinnamon stick. Add just a little water to thin it out a bit; the more water you add, the thinner your sauce will be.

4. Keep in mind that as the mixture simmers, it will thicken. Bring pot to a boil until some of the liquid evaporates, then reduce heat to low, cover, and allow it to simmer.

Sauce 2

Same ingredients and process as the Cashew Nacho Cheese from the Follow Your Heart Bean Burger recipe (see page 22).

Pasta

ground protein (I used Beyond Italian Sausage)
mushrooms
pasta
shredded cheddar cheese (I used Daiya)

1. Chop protein into bite-size pieces and cook along with the sliced mushrooms in a pan on medium heat until well done.

2. Bring water to a boil, add pasta, and cook until al dente—or, in other words, just enough to retain a somewhat firm texture. Be careful not to overcook your pasta, because it will go through another cooking process.

3. When pasta is done, drain and toss into pan with protein and mushrooms.

4. Remove the bay leaves and cinnamon stick from Sauce 1. Then add equal portions of Sauce 1 and 2 until you reach your desired sauciness. Mix well.

5. Baked or stovetop? The choice is yours! If you prefer baked, pour the pasta mixture into an oven-safe pan, top with shredded cheese, and place in a preheated oven at 350 degrees until cheese has melted. For stovetop, toss the shredded cheese on top of your mixture and leave covered allowing the cheese to melt.

6. Plate your pasta and, oh yes, enjoy!

Your Creation

POWER ROLLS

Vibe high on these rolls! They're full of flavor and packed with textures that will take your taste buds on a delicious adventure. The rolls are not your norm, but they are definitely worth exploring. It's a Southern twist on a popular Asian appetizer. Great as a snack or even for lunch with a side salad. You decide!

Energy Work

Your power is within, and everything you create shows your confidence level in that power. How confident are you with your creativity? Are you limiting yourself to your abilities? Are you holding yourself back? Let go, enjoy, and get rewired! This journey is meant to be fun, and variety is the spice of life. Feel like adding something else to your recipe? Just do it! You might surprise yourself. Allow things to flow with ease and comfort.

Roll Ingredients

kale
onion
sweet potatoes
cooking oil
ground protein (I used Beyond Patties)
minced garlic
salt
water
egg roll wraps
cheese (I used Violife Chedder)
dipping sauces (optional)

1. Chop kale, onion, and sweet potatoes into bite-size pieces.
2. Preheat pan with a little oil on medium high. Add your protein and break into crumbles while stirring until done.
3. Mix in the minced garlic and onion. Allow to simmer a bit, then toss in the sweet potatoes. Allow ingredients to cook until potatoes brown a bit.
4. Next, toss in the kale and salt for flavor. Then, add a small amount of water. Cover and allow everything to steam and potatoes to become tender.
5. Once your veggie mixture is done, let it cool before you begin rolling, and also keep in mind that, when frying the rolls, the mixture inside will cook a little bit more.

6. Take a wrap and place a spoonful of the mixture in the middle, then place a piece of cheese on top and roll. Dip your fingers in water and place it along the open edges; this will seal the rolls together. When you have completed rolling all your mixture, allow the rolls to rest a few minutes before frying.

7. Pour enough oil into a pan for the rolls to float. If there's not enough oil, the rolls may stick to the bottom of the pan. Over medium high heat, let your oil get nice and hot, then place rolls into pan. Allow room between them so they cook evenly; flip them over when they become golden brown in color.

8. After rolls have browned on the other side, remove and place them on a wire rack to drain and cool. Once cooled, serve as-is or enjoy them with a dipping sauce of choice.

Your Creation

VIBRANT YELLOW RICE MEDLEY

This rice is full of flavor, super-easy to prepare, and great as a side dish or even by itself. It was created with love and will definitely shine bright however you decide to enjoy it!

Energy Work

This dish is as bright as you are! We tend to eat unconsciously, not even thinking about the food we put into our body. Now is the time to be fully present and aware of each ingredient you are using. Enjoy the process. Take your time and savor the complexities of flavor in each taste while enjoying the company of family, that special one or even yourself. Experience truly being present in the moment; really appreciate it. Know that the energy you pour into the preparation is the same energy that will shine in the finished dish.

Rice Medley

yellow rice
zucchini
onion
yellow and orange peppers
butter (I used Country Crock Plant Butter)

1. To prepare the yellow rice, follow the cooking instructions on the back of the bag. It's best to use the rice the day after preparing to allow the flavor to settle in quite nicely.

2. Wash veggies, pat dry, and then dice them small.

3. Add your butter to a pan on medium heat. Once melted, add your diced veggies and sauté until tender. If you cook the veggies too long, they will be mushy, which will diminish the texture and other components of the dish.

4. If you allowed the rice to sit in the fridge overnight, make sure to reheat it before you add the veggies. Once veggies are done, go ahead and mix them with the rice, and now that everything is all nice and warm, it is ready to serve!

Your Creation

VIBRANT VEGGIE PHILLY

This sandwich is definitely one of a kind, and I guarantee you will not miss the meat! It's bold, vibrant, and delicious—great for lunch, dinner, or on the go. It's also super-quick to prepare and easy for beginners. So, if you've been longing for a traditional Philly cheesesteak, this is what you've been waiting for!

Energy Work

Being in the kitchen should be fun! You should be able to enjoy each and every process. And to make sure that happens, you have to be creative. So with this dish, I want you to step outside the box and utilize some ingredients that aren't on the list. Don't overthink it; just grab something you feel would go great and add to the creation. If you are cooking for the family or someone special, let them taste it and guess what was added other than the ingredients listed. Have fun!

Sandwiches

zucchini
onion
red and yellow peppers
mushrooms
Worcestershire sauce
salt
black pepper
nonstick cooking spray
cheese (I used Chao Vegan Cheese)
whole wheat pita or hoagie roll

1. Chop veggies into thin slices and place in a bowl. Add Worcestershire sauce, salt, and pepper, then toss together, ensuring that the veggies are fully coated.

2. Spray a pan with nonstick cooking spray. Once pan is hot, toss veggies into pan, flipping occasionally until evenly cooked and tender.

3. Remove from heat. Place cheese on top of veggies and cover until cheese has melted.

4. Place pita or hoagie roll in the oven on low heat to slightly toast.

5. Now take your pita or roll, fill it with your mixture, serve, and of course, enjoy!

Your Creation

INSPIRE AND DESIRE TERIYAKI STIR-FRY RICE BOWL

The beautiful colors in this meal are a feast for the eyes! I love Asian-inspired dishes, and this is definitely one of the best. The sauce is so simple, but it's packed with layers of yumminess. This meal is nutrient-dense, so it will keep you full without feeling overstuffed or sluggish.

Energy Work

Before preparing this meal, take a moment to allow the energy around you to flow. This will allow your creativity to shine. Smile, don't overthink it, allow your energy to guide you through this process, and trust in yourself. Know that you and whoever you are cooking with are going to inspire more healthy cooking that makes you feel so good, not only while you're cooking but also while you're eating!

Rice and Vegetables

basmati rice
red and yellow peppers
mushrooms
broccoli
onion
asparagus
nonstick cooking spray

1. First, prepare your rice according to package instructions.

2. While the rice is cooking, prepare your veggies. I prefer to use fresh veggies. If you desire to use frozen, that is totally up to you. So, with that being said, after washing the peppers, mushrooms, and broccoli, chop them along with the onion into desired size. If you'd like this dish to have a traditional Asian appearance and texture, thinly slice your veggies, leaving the broccoli cut into medium pieces.

3. Once you have prepared veggies for the stir-fry, chop off the bottom half of the asparagus spears and toss them out, because they tend to be a little tough to chew.

4. Preheat pan over medium-high heat and coat with the butter spray. When hot, toss in all the veggies except for the asparagus. Stir-fry veggies until tender.

Teriyaki Sauce

soy sauce (I used low-sodium)
brown sugar
garlic powder
ginger powder

1. Preheat saucepan. Add soy sauce, brown sugar, garlic powder, and ginger powder.

2. Let the sauce reduce (simmer slowly) until it thickens; for a thicker sauce, add more brown sugar and bring to a boil.

Stir-fry

1. Once the sauce has reached your desired consistency, add it to the pan with the veggies, reduce the heat to low, and toss the veggies in the sauce, making sure they are well coated.

2. While the veggies and sauce finish cooking, place the asparagus spears in the preheated pan coated with cooking spray. Allow them to cook until tender.

3. Once the asparagus is done, serve the veggies and sauce over the rice and enjoy!

Your Creation

GALAXY CHOCOLATE BANANA STRAWBERRY PANCAKES

Did somebody say, "Dessert for breakfast?" The whole family will enjoy these pancakes; they're sweet but not too sweet and super-simple to make. Great if you're planning a brunch or for breakfast on Saturday or any day, these will even make a delicious dessert that everyone will love! The light and fluffy tasty treats shine bright like a diamond, so don't be surprised when they quickly become a weekend go-to.

Energy Work

Balance is key. Create a form of balance in your kitchen by letting go of any fear-based preconceived notions about the meal you have chosen to prepare. Allow yourself to be open to the entire process from beginning to end. Place your intentions on how much you enjoy preparing and combining the ingredients and how good and satisfying your meal is going to taste once it is finished.

Pancakes

oats
ripe bananas
almond milk
allspice
baking powder
vanilla
apple cider vinegar
nonstick spray

1. Let's start with the base. Take your oats and grind them into a powder using a high-power blender or food processor.

2. Once oats are in powder form, add the bananas, almond milk, and allspice, making sure you don't add too much milk. Remember, this is a pancake batter, not a crêpe. My advice would be to add a little bit of milk at a time until it reaches a medium thickness.

3. Once this is done, add your baking powder, vanilla, and apple cider vinegar. Keep in mind you don't need to use much of these ingredients. The vanilla is for flavor, and the other two will help the pancake to rise.

4. Once the batter is your desired consistency, it's time to cook! Don't be afraid to taste your batter; there are no raw eggs, so it is totally safe. Preheat pan over medium-high heat, coat well with a nonstick spray, then pour desired amount of batter into pan. When the pancake batter begins to bubble, it's time to flip. Once the pancake becomes golden brown on the other side, it's done.

Sauce

dried dates
water
cacao powder
strawberries

1. Place the dried dates in a bowl of hot water. Allow them to soak until they have -softened, then drain.

2. Bring a small amount of water to a boil, then slowly add the cacao powder while stirring mixture continuously, watching for thickness. If sauce is too runny, add more cacao to the pot.

3. Once you have the desired consistency, pour your mixture into the blender and toss in the dates for sweetness. Thoroughly blend the ingredients together until smooth, then it's done!

4. Now, plate the pancakes top with sliced strawberries or anything you choose. Drizzle with your delicious sauce and enjoy!

Your Creation

HIGH VIBEZ TACOS WITH JALAPEÑO MANGO SALSA

Trust me, these tacos are bangin'! They're high in protein and have the perfect amount of sweetness to balance the spice. The layers of delicious flavors will definitely put you in the vibe! The tacos are easy to prep, and you can have them ready to go when you are.

Energy Work

Feel free to read this affirmation out loud or to yourself. This meal that I have chosen to prepare shall be satisfying to my heart and pleasing to my palate, and all that I eat and drink will be assimilated by my body for my good. And so, it is!

Taco Filling

dry black beans or canned chickpeas
onion
firm tofu
cumin powder
salt
garlic powder
coriander powder
smoked paprika
nonstick cooking spray

1. If using dry beans, soak them overnight, rinse thoroughly, then put in a size-appropriate pot.

2. Finely dice your onion, then place in a large bowl suitable for mixing all of the ingredients for your taco meat.

3. Cover beans with cool water, place the lid on the pot, and allow to boil until tender. When beans are done, drain and place in the bowl with your onion. Using a fork, gently mash them; you want to keep some of the texture to the beans. (If you prefer to use canned chickpeas, rinse and drain them well, then gently mash with a fork.)

4. Drain tofu and chop into small pieces. Using a paper towel, press down to remove any excess water, then add tofu to the beans. The ideal ratio is more beans than tofu.

5. Now, to your mixture, add cumin, salt, garlic, coriander, and smoked paprika. Once seasonings are added, mix together well.

6. Preheat pan over medium-high heat, coating with your choice of oil cooking spray. Once pan is hot, add bean mixture and let cook until you see a slightly crispy coating appear.

Jalapeño Mango Salsa

jalapeño
mango
onion
cilantro
salt

1. Chop the jalapeño, mango, onion, and cilantro into chunks.
2. In a blender or food processor, pulse your chopped veggies until mixture reaches the texture you prefer your salsa to be, then add a pinch of salt to flavor if you like.

High Vibez Tacos

corn tortillas
chopped kale
diced tomato

1. Once your taco filling and salsa are done, preheat a pan to warm your tortillas and prepare to plate your tacos.
2. Place tortillas on a plate. Add the taco filling along with some chopped kale and diced tomato. Then top it all with your delicious, homemade salsa. *Hora de comer*!

Your Creation

_____

_____

_____

_____

_____

_____

_____

_____

_____

_____

_____

_____

_____

_____

_____

_____

_____

_____

_____

_____

ALPHA AND OMEGA CHICKEN CHOW MEIN

Craving some Chinese takeout? Try this chicken chow mein—you won't regret it. It has all the flavor, minus all the unnecessary additives and fats. This dish can be made in one pan and feeds the whole family. Adding extra veggies is one of my favorite little tricks to keep my tummy full; not only are they very tasty, but they are also low in calories. This is just the beginning of your preparing Chinese food at home and the end of ordering takeout!

Energy Work

Feel free to repeat this affirmation out loud or to yourself. I believe in myself and in my ability to enter my kitchen and create meals that will quickly become the favorites of my family and friends. I believe that there is nothing missing. I know I have everything I need to masterfully prepare this dish. I believe in the process; now, let's do this!

Chow Mein

carrots
onion
bok choy
fresh or frozen broccoli
yellow peppers
nonstick cooking spray
fresh ginger
fresh garlic
protein (I used Gardein chicken strips)
udon noodles
Szechuan sauce (I used House of Tsang Szechuan Spicy Sauce)

1. Chop all veggies into desired size and place in a large bowl.
2. Coat wok or large pan with the oil you prefer and preheat over medium-high heat.
3. While pan is preheating, mince ginger and garlic, then add to the pan. Toss ginger and garlic around just a bit, then add the protein, allowing it to brown slightly.
4. Once your protein has browned, add veggies along with your protein and udon noodles. Gently toss all of your ingredients together before adding the sauce. Give it a little taste, because some sauces are salty or spicier than others. This way, you don't overdo it.
5. Mix again, making sure everything is evenly coated, then reduce heat. Cover the pan and allow the ingredients to steam. This process does not take long at all. Remember, the longer you allow them to steam, the softer your veggies will be, and we don't want that.
6. Once everything is done, plate and enjoy!

Your Creation

COSMIC BLACK BEAN CHILI CHEESE FRIES

These fries are out of this world! All the cheesy goodness, minus the guilt. And get this: it's served over a bed of crispy, delicious sweet potato fries. This recipe is definitely outside of the box, so I'm sure you're wondering … how are these chili cheese fries guilt-free? Well, this cheese is made from potatoes and carrots. Yep, surprised, aren't you? Well, let's get started!

Energy Work

K.I.S.S.—Keep It Simple, Sugar! There is beauty in simplicity, and there is nothing more natural than to think about something you would like to eat and then, like magic, all of the perfect combinations of ingredients come to mind. Before you know it, your masterpiece is on the table, and all because you kept it simple!

Chili Beans

black beans (canned or dry)
chopped onion
garlic
cumin
cayenne pepper
salt
coriander
smoked paprika

1. For dry beans, soak overnight, rinse, then place in a pot covered with cool water. You can also follow the directions on the back of the bag if you like.

2. Add the chopped onion, garlic, cumin, cayenne, salt, coriander, and paprika to the pot. Cover and let beans cook until tender, stirring occasionally, over medium heat. (If you choose to use canned beans, pour beans into a pot, add the same ingredients, and allow beans to heat over medium-low heat.)

Cheese Sauce

brown potatoes
carrots
jalapeño rings
nutritional yeast
veggie broth

1. Wash and peel potatoes and carrots. Place in a pot, cover with water, and boil until nice and tender. Once done, drain the water, then add potatoes and carrots to your blender along with jalapeño rings and nutritional yeast.

2. Add a little veggie broth at a time until sauce reaches the consistency you desire. Give it a taste and, if necessary, add more nutritional yeast to give it that cheesy flavor, along with a pinch of salt if needed.

3. Pour your cheese sauce in a nonstick pan. Simmer on low heat to keep warm until the chili beans and fries are ready.

Sweet Potato Fries

sweet potatoes
nonstick cooking spray

1. Wash sweet potatoes and towel-dry. Then slice into your desired thickness.

2. Spray your cookie sheet and potatoes with nonstick cooking spray. Add potatoes to cookie sheet and bake at 350 degrees until crispy. If you prefer to use your air fryer, then do your thing!

Chili Cheese Fries

sour cream or other toppings
vegan sour cream

Now that everything is done, plate your sweet potato fries, top with chili, then some of that delicious cheese sauce, and add a dollop of sour cream or any other topping you choose. Be creative!

Your Creation

SYNERGY TROPICAL YOGURT BOWL

Quick, fast, and easy for when you're on the go! This bowl will provide you with all the energy you need. It was created when I needed a change from my routine but wanted to make sure I was getting enough nutrients and fuel to complete my workout afterward. So yes, this can be breakfast or a protein snack before or after the gym.

Energy Work

What if my only objective was to have fun? What if I engaged everyone I encountered at the market to have fun with me? What if I had fun while prepping my dish? What if every time I tasted my creation, it made me smile, it made me giggle, and it made me feel so good? Then I hereby decree that having fun is to be incorporated into preparing every meal, every day!

Yogurt Bowl

banana
pineapple
frozen berries mix
plain yogurt (I used vegan)
protein powder (I used vegan vanilla protein)
walnuts
pumpkin seeds

1. Chop fruit into bite-sized pieces, place in a bowl, and set aside.

2. Add the yogurt and one scoop of protein powder to a serving bowl.

3. Mix yogurt and protein powder together, then top with fruit and nuts. All done, now enjoy!

Your Creation

About the Author

Mind Body And Soul Coach Laura Calbert is all about creating ease and flow which she believes anyone can obtain with the right tools. At 407lbs Laura experienced confusion, difficulty, and stagnant energy preventing her from experiencing the life she knew she deserved. She had struggled with these things for majority of her life. Laura knew that it was time to take her life back and begin her journey towards health and wellness. In 2016 Laura began her journey of transforming her mind so her body would align. As she has stated in PEOPLE magazine and The Today Show, Laura knew she had work to do, but she believed that once she rebuilt that connection with her inner self and began to trust her again, she would succeed. Ease and Flow cookbook shows its readers that they have the ability to create exactly what they desire, not only in the kitchen, but within their lives!

Printed in the United States
by Baker & Taylor Publisher Services